ED SHEERAN

REAL BiOS

By Marie Morreale

Children's Press®
An Imprint of Scholastic Inc.
New York Toronto London Auckland Sydney
Mexico City New Delhi Hong Kong
Danbury, Connecticut

Photographs ©: AP Images: 1, 45 (Charles Sykes/Invision), 41 top (Dave Allocca, Starpix), 36 (Evan Agostini/Invision), 40 top (Mark Pokorny, Warner Bros. Pictures), 42 (Owen Sweeney/Invision), 2, 3 (Press Association); Dreamstime/Featureflash: 33; Everett Collection/Paramount Pictures: 15 bottom right; Getty Images: 6, 7 (Axelle/Bauer-Griffin), 16, 18 bottom, 19 (Christie Goodwin), 22 (Christopher Polk), back cover, 7 inset (Dave J Hogan), 23 bottom (Ethan Miller), 18 top (Eugene Gologursky), 28 (Gareth Cattermole/TAS), 10 (Greetsia Tent), 12 (Jewel Samad), 20 top, 24 top (Kevin Mazur), 23 top (Kevin Mazur/Fox), 24 bottom (Kevin Winter), 8 (Larry Busacca/TAS), cover (Larry Marano), 39 (Mathis Wienand), 25 (NBC), 29 (Robyn Beck), 20 bottom (Shirlaine Forrest); iStockphoto: 15 top (ivanastar), 15 bottom left (Nicolas McComber); Newscom: 14 (Darren Eagles/Zumapress), 32 (Diggzy, PacificCoastNews), 27 (Paul Martinka/Splash News); REX USA/Jesse Wild/Future Publishing/Rex: 35; Shutterstock, Inc.: 13 bottom (cinema-festival), 13 top, 37 center left, 37 bottom (Featureflash), 38 (Geoffrey Jones), 37 center right, 38 (Helga Esteb), 41 bottom (Lipskiy), 40 bottom (Melinda Fawver), 35 inset (Oksana Kuzmina), 37 top (s_bukley), 34 (Venus Angel); Thinkstock: 13 center (sumnersgraphicsinc); Zuma Press: 30 (Brian Jordan/Retna Pictures B282), 9 (Fontaine), 4, 5 (Igor Vidyashev).

Library of Congress Cataloging-in-Publication Data
Morreale, Marie.
   Ed Sheeran / by Marie Morreale.
      pages cm. — (Real bios)
   Includes bibliographical references and index.
   ISBN 978-0-531-21199-1 (lib. bdg. : alk. paper) —
ISBN 978-0-531-21274-5 (pbk. : alk. paper)
   1. Sheeran, Ed, 1991——Juvenile literature. 2. Singers—England—Biography—Juvenile literature. I. Title.
   ML3930.S484M67 2013
   782.42164092—dc23 [B]   2014004444

Printed in the United States of America 113
SCHOLASTIC, CHILDREN'S PRESS, and associated logos are trademarks and/or registered trademarks of Scholastic Inc.

1 2 3 4 5 6 7 8 9 10 R 24 23 22 21 20 19 18 17 16 15

Ed performs at the British Teenage Cancer Trust charity concert.

MEET ED!

HE HAS THE MUSICAL MAGIC TOUCH!

n the glitzy and glamorous world of pop music, no one would have ever predicted that Ed Sheeran, with his boy-next-door ooks and shy-guy personality, would become a major, massive negastar. But he did! Ed is part of the 21st century British nvasion of music acts, and he is friends with many of his fellow British superstars, including One Direction, Little Mix, and Olly Murs. He also has fans—nicknamed Sheerios—all over the globe.

In this book, you will find fascinating facts about Ed, such as the way he was bullied as a little boy because he was a "ginger" (British slang for redhead), and how he is a superfan of the Hobbit book and movie series. He even has one of the swords from *The Hobbit: The Desolation of Smaug*! There are also dozens of fabulous photos and cool quotes. Included arc all the deets you need to know about Ed Sheeran—an absolute must-read!

CONTENTS

A Toronto audience lets Ed know they are Lego fans, too!

ED SHEERAN—

GINGER POWER!

HE WRITES THE SONGS & SINGS THE SONGS

Ed Sheeran grew up in a very creative household in Framlingham, England. His mom, Imogen, is a jewelry designer, and his dad, John, is an art **curator** and lecturer. But it wasn't just art that influenced the Sheerans—music was very important, too. Ed's older brother, Matthew, became a classical music composer. Of course, the youngest Sheeran became one of the world's most popular singer/songwriters.

But let's back up a minute. We know who Ed Sheeran is today, but what was his childhood like? Well, if you ask Ed, he would tell you there were a few negatives—he had poor eyesight and a hearing problem in one ear. He was also bullied for having red hair. But his family was close and supportive. He liked to hang out with his friends at

Early on, Ed considered becoming an actor, but music won out. Yay!

Just Ed
"I'm not very materialistic."

Ed lends his voice— and Teddy bear—to a Children in Need Rocks charity event.

Dressed as a clown, Ed surprises Taylor Swift in Nashville, TN—the last concert of her U.S. Red tour.

school, listen to music, sing in the church choir, and make people laugh. That trait probably came from his mom. She was very inventive when it came to encouraging her children to work on their talents and not be afraid to be different. That included their choice of toys. "I remember during the yo-yo craze my mum wouldn't spend eight pounds and [instead] made me one out of jam jar lids and string," Ed explained to contactmusic .com. "Can you imagine taking that to school? But now I see it was cool and I realize how amazing my parents are for not giving me that stuff."

Ideal Weekend

"Sitting in my flat [apartment], in sweatpants, watching a DVD. . . . As long as there are chips —well, French fries, as you call them! And pizza, fried chicken, wings [and] Doritos!"

Ed developed a wicked sense of humor, but he wasn't the class clown. He always had something funny to say, though. Maybe that was his way of dealing with the school bullies.

"I think everyone goes through a bit of bullying at school. Of course you get picked on for certain things . . . ," Ed told the Australian radio/TV show *Take 40*. "I was quite a weird kid when

Ed . . . deep in thought. Wonder if he's working on a new song?

"BEING GINGER CAN SEEM LIKE A BAD THING WHEN YOU'RE YOUNG. . . . [BUT] I HAVE COME OUT THE OTHER END [OF BULLYING]— AND BLOSSOMED."

I was little: I wore big glasses, had hearing problems, had a stutter, and I had ginger hair!"

One thing that helped Ed deal with the bullying was his love of music and acting. For a while, Ed wasn't sure which one he was going to pursue as a career. Music was his first love. He told the *Edinburgh Evening News*, "I first picked up a guitar when I was 10 or 11. I picked up a few **chords** and quite quickly started writing my own songs using other people's chord structures."

It was a chance meeting with his musical idol, Irish singer/songwriter Damien Rice, that really made 11-year-old Ed think seriously about music as a possible

Irish singer/songwriter Damien Rice was Ed's first musical influence.

life choice. Ed and his parents had gone to a Damien Rice show. Afterward, they ended up in the same restaurant as the singer. "I had a little bit of a chat and kind of had an epiphany, like, 'Wow, this is exactly what I want to do!'" Ed told London newspaper *The Telegraph*. "I got right home that night and wrote a whole bunch of songs. I remember one was called 'Typical Average Teen.' Yeah, I was one of those."

But then for a brief time in his early teens, Ed flirted with pursuing an acting career. "This e-mail came through saying, 'If you can sing, play the guitar and act, then audition for this. I thought, 'This sounds like me,'" he told London's *Daily Mirror*.

The e-mail was an invitation to audition for England's National Youth Theatre. The National Youth Theatre is a charitable organization that selects 500 kids to take part in a summer program for acting and theatrical technical courses. "I went for it and there was a two-week audition period where they filmed lots of stuff," Ed said. "I got down to the final three. . . . I said to myself that if I get this, I'll give up music and concentrate on acting. Luckily, I realized it wasn't for me and I didn't get it anyway."

Strict Allowance
"My manager doesn't let me have credit cards as I do weird things. He has to approve everything I buy."

Ed turned back to music. He told contactmusic.com that he realized, "I can hold a tune, but my acting is not quite up to the same standard yet." It was the right choice. "By the time I was 14 or so, I thought music was something I'd like to do, and then by 16 I started to think it was something I could do," Ed told the *Edinburgh Evening News.* "That's when I took all the big risks."

His major risk was leaving school when he was only 17 and moving to London to pursue his dream of becoming a singer. "[My parents] were

FACT FILE

THE BASICS

Designer Hoodie

"I wore a hoodie to the Olympics closing ceremony, but it was a Ralph Lauren hoodie!"

LL NAME Edward
ristopher Sheeran

CKNAMES Ed, Teddy

RTHDAY
bruary 17, 1991

STROLOGICAL SIGN
quarius

IRTHPLACE Halifax, West
orkshire, England

CHILDHOOD HOME Framlingham,
Suffolk, England

CURRENT HOMES A farm in
Framlingham, Suffolk, England,
and a house in Hendersonville,
Tennessee, which is near
Nashville

PARENTS Imogen Lock and
John Sheeran

SIBLING Older brother,
Matthew

HERITAGE Irish and
English

PETS A cat named Bellini
(with ginger hair!) and a
Labrador retriever
named Spinee

HIGH SCHOOL Thomas Mills High School

MUSICAL INFLUENCES Bob Dylan, Van
Morrison, Eminem, Damien Rice, Stevie
Wonder

BEST 1D PAL:
Harry Styles

CELEBRITY CRUSH
Emma Stone

WARDROBE MUST Hoodies

FASHION OOPS Ed
was named Worst
Dressed Man by
GQ magazine
in 2012

SUPERPOWER
Invisibility—"I'd just
chill out and watch DVDs at home
while everyone thinks I've
disappeared."

BIGGEST FEAR Heights

SPECIAL CHARITIES Crisis and
Bluebell Wood Children's Hospice

FANS' NICKNAME Sheerios

TWITTER @edsheeran

really supportive of my music in that they allowed me to drop out of school and move out of our home, which not many parents would do," he explained to *TeenVogue* magazine. Even though Ed stopped going to school, he still found time to study and earn a degree.

When he arrived in London, Ed started playing **gigs** wherever he could. He played 312 shows in 2009, sometimes to as few as five people and sometimes to no one at all. Ed was on a mission to get people to hear his music. And that he did!

FACT FILE

FAVORITES

"I'VE REMAINED RELATIVEL[Y] NORMAL. I'M STILL WEARING THE SAME KIND OF CLOTHES AND I'M STIL[L] WITH THE SAME FRIENDS.

...AME Lego (he loves to
...ay with 1D's Harry Styles)

...MERICAN FAST-FOOD RESTAURANT
...-N-Out Burger

...MEXICAN RESTAURANT Chipotle

...CHICKEN RESTAURANT Nando's

...OAST SPREAD Marmite

...BRITISH MEAL Fish and chips and mushy
...peas with tartar sauce

CONDIMENT Heinz ketchup

MEAL TO COOK Fajitas with noodles

CANDY Twix

SODA Coca-Cola

INSTRUMENT Guitar

SONG TO PERFORM "Give Me Love"

1990S TV SERIES Buffy the Vampire
Slayer

FAN GIFT Doughnuts decorated with
Lord of the Rings Lego figures

DISNEY MOVIES The Hunchback of
Notre Dame and Pocahontas

COLOR Blue

EXERCISE Hiking

ANIMAL Cat

CARTOON CAT
Puss in Boots

ANIMATED MOVIE
Shrek

"I THINK I'VE BEEN AROUND FOR A WHILE. BUT I STILL HAVE TO PAY MY DUES."

THE ED SHOW

A BRITISH BOY MAKES THE WORLD SING

By the time Ed Sheeran was 17 years old, he had moved to London, signed with a management team, made a name in the local music scene, and worked constantly. During those days, he told *People* magazine, he had "dreams of selling records and playing in stadiums." Even before his London days, Ed had already laid the groundwork. In 2005, when he was 15 years old, he recorded his first independent **EP**, *The Orange Room*. In 2006 he released his second EP, *Ed Sheeran*, and in 2007 he came out with his third EP, *Want Some?*

His music—a blend of folk, pop, and hip-hop accompanied by an acoustic guitar—was winning an audience in England. Most importantly, music company executives were becoming

Chart Champ
Ed's debut album, +, debuted on the Billboard Top 200 chart at number five—the highest ever for a British male artist!

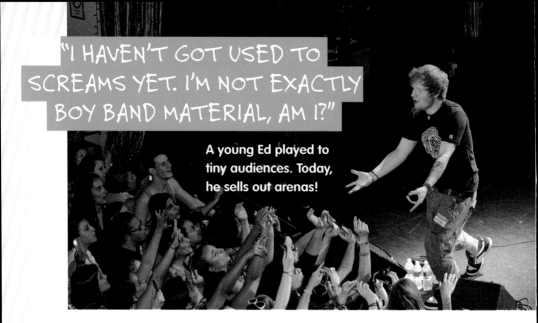

"I HAVEN'T GOT USED TO SCREAMS YET. I'M NOT EXACTLY BOY BAND MATERIAL, AM I?"

A young Ed played to tiny audiences. Today, he sells out arenas!

aware of this young, multitalented artist. He toured with a number of underground British musicians and continued to release independent EPs. In 2010, he came out with *Loose Change*, which featured his international debut single, "The A Team."

Ed decided to take another big risk in 2010. He left his management company and bought a round-trip ticket to Los Angeles, California. He "couch-crashed" with friends

Follow Ed's

Amazing Journey

JANUARY 1, 2005
Ed's first independent EP, *The Orange Room*, is released.

JANUARY 2011
Ed signs with a major record label.

because he didn't have the money to stay in a hotel or rent an apartment. Ed had one guaranteed gig, and it was at an open-mic night. Newbies to the music scene often play open-mic gigs at L.A. clubs. Even though artists are rarely paid for these shows, these gigs are an opportunity to be seen and heard. It paid off for Ed. "There's always small opportunities for people to get up, especially if you've just got a guitar and you can plug in and play," Ed explained to *The Telegraph*. After that show, Ed was offered more club dates. He even performed at actor/singer Jamie Foxx's club The Foxxhole. Foxx was so impressed that he made an amazing offer to Ed. "Jamie said, 'I have a house with a studio, it was built for people like

Keep on Trying

"Success is the best revenge for anything, keep ya head down and work hard to achieve," Ed tweeted to his fans!

APRIL 7, 2011
Ed's first digital EP for Atlantic Records, *One Take EP,* is released.

JUNE 12, 2011
"The A Team," the first single from Ed's debut album, is released.

SEPTEMBER 12, 2011
Ed's debut album + is released in Europe.

NOVEMBER 11, 2011
"Lego House," from Ed's + album, is released.

Ed performs "The A Team" with icon Elton John at the 2013 Grammys. Wow!

you, come and stay on my sofa and just make music,'" Ed told *The Telegraph*. "It was really surreal."

Ed accepted Jamie's offer. He worked and slept at the superstar's private recording studio. He made good use of his time in L.A., and his fan base was growing fast. YouTube helped a lot, as did the fact that Ed continued to self-release EPs—including 2010's *Ed Sheeran: Live at the Bedford* and *Songs I Wrote With Amy*, and 2011's

FEBRUARY 21, 2012 Ed receives two BRIT Awards—Best British Male Solo Artist and British Breakthrough of the Year.

JUNE 4, 2012 Ed performs "The A Team" at the United Kingdom's Diamond Jubilee of Queen Elizabeth II.

JUNE 12, 2012 Ed's debut album + is released in North America.

No. 5 Collaborations Project. It was *Collaborations* that really clicked with fans, and the record reached number two on the iTunes charts.

Things really began happening for Ed in 2011. First, he signed with pop legend Elton John's management company, Rocket Music Entertainment Group. "They're just wicked—they're like, 'You do your thing and we'll do our thing and we'll meet in the middle,' rather than telling me what to play, what to wear and what to sing," Ed told *Billboard* magazine.

That was totally different from the music industry executives who had showed interest in Ed earlier. "About five years ago, a lot of people were saying I had to change me look and sound," Ed revealed to *Teen Vogue*.

> "[THE U.S. HAS] BEEN VERY POSITIVE. . . . THE FANS ARE ALL REALLY NICE, AND I SEE THEM AFTER EVERY GIG."

AUGUST 12, 2012
Ed sings Pink Floyd's "Wish You Were Here" at the London Olympics closing ceremony.

FEBRUARY 10, 2013
Ed attends the Grammys and performs a duet of "The A Team" with Elton John.

MARCH 13, 2013
Ed joins Taylor Swift as her opening act for the North American leg of her Red tour.

MAY 19, 2013
Ed performs "Lego House" at the 2013 *Billboard* Music Awards.

Elton John sure wasn't telling Ed to change anything. He became one of Ed's biggest fans and even took the young singer under his wing. Elton knows talent, that's for sure!

After that, Ed signed a recording contract with a major record company. He told a BBC *Blast* reporter that he was surprised by the offer. "I got a call one day saying that a girl who was a junior in the record company has heard your stuff, she sent it up to the head and he'd like to fly you over [to the United States]. It was the best news."

Though Ed was just out of his teens, he was already signed to important management and record companies. It was too good to be true! But Ed didn't let his good fortune go to his head. He continued working hard on his singing

Sweet Tweet
"Today is the final day of the @TaylorSwift13 RED tour, 6 months, 66 shows and a combined audience of 1.3 million. So much fun."

JULY 12, 2013
Ed performs at *The Today Show*'s 18th Annual Summer Concert Series at Rockefeller Plaza.

AUGUST 11, 2013
Ed wins Choice Music Breakout Artist at the Teen Choice Awards.

OCTOBER 14 & 15, 2013 Ed is a mentor for Christina Aguilera's team on *The Voice*.

Besties Ed Sheeran and 1D's Harry Styles have a backstage moment at the 2013 Teen Choice Awards.

and songwriting. Finally, in June 2012, Ed released his debut album, +, in the United States. It immediately climbed to the top of the iTunes charts. When Ed heard the news, he tweeted, "Oh my word! My album is #1 on USA iTunes!,!,!! so happy right now. And Canada!,!,!, Getting emotional right now, gonna eat some nachos."

OCTOBER 29, 2013
Ed sells out his first Madison Square Garden concert as a **headliner** in the first of three shows at Madison Square Garden—he appears there on November 1st and 7th, too.

DECEMBER 13, 2013
The Hobbit: The Desolation of Smaug is released—Ed's song "I See Fire" is featured in the film and released as a single.

Ed poses for a "snap" with Justin Bieber at the NYC Z100 Jingle Ball 2012.

America was finally getting a taste of Ed Sheeran—actually, more than just a taste. Ed was an early collaborator with One Direction. He first met 1D's Harry Styles while he was couch-crashing at a mutual friend's London flat. They instantly became **mates**. The **lads** from One Direction were early supporters of Ed's, and they asked him to appear at several of their concerts in Europe. He even wrote "Moments," "Little Things," "Over Again," and "Summer Love" for their first two albums, *Up All Night* and *Take Me Home*. Ed also

JANUARY 26, 2014
Nominated for Best New Artist, Ed attends the 2014 Grammys.

MARCH 4, 2014
"Sing"—the first single from Ed's second album is released.

collaborated with Taylor Swift for the single and video for "Everything Has Changed," from her album *Red*. He has worked with artists such as Justin Bieber, Lupe Fiasco, Pharrell Williams, and many more. Of course, Ed eventually had to think of his own work. He told MTV News, "I've written a lot of songs and a lot of them are getting placed at the moment with different acts.

"THERE'S NO KEY TO SUCCESS, BUT THE KEY TO FAILURE IS TRYING TO PLEASE EVERYONE. SO . . . I'M GOING TO KEEP DOING WHAT I WANT TO DO."

. . . But as far as writing fresh songs, right now the Taylor thing was an exception because I think she's great. But right now I can only concentrate on writing stuff for me."

Ed did take time off from working on new music to appear at the closing ceremony of the London 2012 Summer Olympics. He sang Pink Floyd's classic "Wish You Were Here," and he tweeted that it was "the gig of a

APRIL 12, 2014
Ed performs his new song, "Don't," on *Saturday Night Live*.

JUNE 23, 2014
Ed releases his second album, *x*.

AUGUST 22, 2014
Ed opens his arena tour in Seattle, Washington.

lifetime!" Of course, he hadn't been on the road with Taylor Swift yet. In March 2013, Ed began playing as the opening act on Taylor's Red tour. Not only did he have an amazing time on tour, but he also realized it was an important career move. "I think Taylor's just opening a lot of doors and it's up to me to make sure that I get through them," he told MTV News. "It's a massive opportunity for me and I want to make sure to grab it with both hands. . . . It will be exciting to be back in a situation where I'm playing in front of people who are complete strangers and I have to win them over."

Actually, Ed was already winning over his audience. He was nominated for the 2013 Grammy Song of the Year for "The A Team." And though he didn't win the award (fun.'s "We Are Young" won), he did get to perform with his mentor Elton John. According to Ed, that made him a winner! "[Elton] put it together," he told MTV News. "He rung me up one day and said, 'How would you feel about performing with me at the Grammys?' I was like, 'I'll check my schedule.'"

Of course, it "fit in" with his schedule. At the Grammys, Ed was already thinking of his next album. "I've got around 26 songs for the next record and I've got another nine months on the road to keep writing as well," he told *Billboard*. "So the record's definitely on its way."

For the next few months, while he was opening for Taylor Swift, Ed was also writing and recording his second album. By the time the Red tour was half over, Ed was already itching to release his sophomore album. He wasn't quite ready to do that yet, but he wasn't above teasing about it a bit. He told reporters that people might be surprised by his new direction. He joked with MTV News, "It's probably closer to a hip-hop record to be honest, at the moment, but who knows, it might turn into a rap-metal record?!"

Later on, he got a little more serious and told *Hollywood Life*, "It's not an album about fame and fortune; it's an album about relationships."

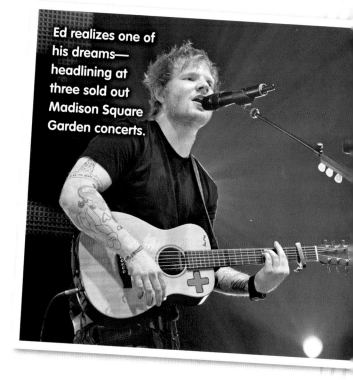

Ed realizes one of his dreams— headlining at three sold out Madison Square Garden concerts.

Ed spent the rest of 2013 on the go, go, go. He opened for the 66 concerts on Taylor's Red tour. He accepted the 2013 Teen Choice Award for Music

Taylor-Made

Taylor Swift first let Ed know she was a fan when she wrote lyrics from his song "Lego House" on her arm during her Speak Now tour. Then she e-mailed him to say she was a fan and ask, "Should we write a song?" He instantly said YES! Next thing he knew, he was visiting Taylor's Nashville home. The pair got to work right away on writing "Everything Has Changed." "We wrote the song on a trampoline, ate some apple pie and had a jam," Ed told *Rolling Stone* magazine. "It was very fun. It came in 20 minutes, really. It was a really simple song to write. We just had two guitars and strummed it out."

Breakout Artist. He joined Christina Aguilera as a team mentor on *The Voice*. He sold out tickets for his October and November concerts at Madison Square Garden in three minutes—the tickets were in such demand, Ed had to add a third show. He was photographed with Elmo, Oscar the Grouch, and Cookie Monster when he taped a *Sesame Street* episode to be aired in 2014. He threw a Halloween night party and gig at New York City's Mercury Lounge—Ed went as a gingerbread man. He wrote "I See Fire" for the soundtrack of *The Hobbit: The Desolation of maug*, which was released n December. He celebrated Thanksgiving Eve and Thanksgiving Day at Jennifer Aniston's and Courtney Cox's houses. He was nominated for Best New Artist for the 56th annual Grammy Awards—his reaction was "Oh, yikes!"

Ed may not have won the Grammy, but he made his Sheerios proud . . . and more anxious than ever to hear his new music! Never

Ed couldn't wait to go to the premiere of *The Hobbit: The Desolation of Smaug.*

one to disappoint, in March 2014 Ed released "Sing," the first single from his second album. On June 23, 2014, Ed's new album, *x* [pronounced "multiply"], hit the record stores, iTunes, Amazon, and more. You can bet his Sheerios count is going to multiply!

"I JUST LIKE WRITING PERSONAL SONGS THAT MEAN SOMETHING TO ME. . . . THEY ALL COME FROM THE SAME PLACE AND HAVE A STORY AND MEANING BEHIND THEM."

Selfie Time! Ed makes a fan's day. Sheerios always come first!

ED TAKES ANY & ALL QUESTIONS

CHECK OUT HIS ANSWERS

Accordng to reporters and journalists who have had him in front of a microphone, interviewing Ed Sheeran is a lot of fun. Somewhat quiet and very good-natured, Ed seems to turn every Q&A into a laugh-a-thon. Always smiling and willing to follow the interviewer's lead— even when he was interviewed by a cat named Monty— Ed is really enjoying himself right now. The great thing is that he hasn't changed from the lad down the lane that he was before he became one of the biggest artists in the world. You just have to love him!

On performing and being up for an award at the 2013 Grammys . . . "I was most nervous about the awards I was up for. The performing side of things is quite exhilarating, knowing I was performing in front of the whole world, the whole industry. I know it sounds silly but I didn't really have one of those star-struck

Ed always stops to sign autographs for his true-blue Sheerios!

moments that night—it was all a bit kind of a full-on with the whole thing."

On the weirdest place he ever wrote a song . . .
"Probably the [bathroom]. I remember I was at a venue backstage. It was quite a small venue, and there was nowhere for me to go, so I locked myself in the [bathroom] and wrote a song."

On his 24/7 schedule . . . "I never really need breaks. I mean, it's always nice to see the family and friends at Christmas, and other holidays, but I've always been a bit of a nomad and I'm just constantly traveling and working. I love it! I can seriously say that I have the best job in the world!"

On being a cat person . . . "I grew up with cats, and I'm definitely a cat person; dogs don't like me much. Actually, my granddad had bulldogs when I was younger, and me and the dogs just didn't get along."

On Taylor Swift's cat, Meredith . . . "Meredith doesn't like anyone. There are moments when she doesn't even like Taylor! She's just a very ungrateful cat. She just expects you to come to her and if [you don't], then she'll just glare at you. . . . I think [because] Taylor isn't a diva, I think someone in that camp needs to be a diva. So Meredith fits that quite well."

After a few months on tour with Taylor, things changed a bit. "[Meredith and I] get along. She won't hang out with the dancers—but she'll come and hang out with me."

On how he got Harry Potter actor Rupert Grint to be in his "Lego House" video . . .

"I connected with him through Tom Felton who plays Draco in the films. He was a fan and we were talking a bit, and I pulled a favor, and he got Rupert to do it, which I'm really grateful for."

THE GINGER GUY'S SCRAPBOOK OF LIFE

ED ON CATS, GUITARS, FRIENDS & MORE

ED'S GUITARS

Believe it or not, Ed names them! "I've got James the second, I've got Trevor, I've got Keith, I've got Lloyd, I've got Nigel, Cyril and Felix," he told *The Sun*. "It started off with really awkward names like Lloyd, but now I name them after my team. My lighting guy was called James and the guitar James broke so now I've got James the second, my guitar check is called Trevor."

STAR TALK

ED'S CELEB FRIENDS LOVE HIM!

Taylor Swift:
"[Ed's] hilarious. I've kind of thought this before—how he's a strange combination of being like an eight-year-old child and an 80-year-old. Because . . . he plays with Lego and stuff and then he also has the best advice you ever ask for. So he's like the perfect combination of both ends of the spectrum age-wise."

Elton John:

"Ed Sheeran phoned me up and said he'd got the choice between doing another record or going on the Taylor Swift tour in America. I told him it was a no-brainer—you go on the Taylor Swift tour….you do all these dates and you may be driven crazy by it in the end, but the experience and exposure you'll get . . . well, you just can't buy that."

Louis Tomlinson:

"Ed is phenomenal. He's been one of the artists who has blown up in a major way."

Demi Lovato:

"Lately I've been listening to a lot of Ed Sheeran. . . . That's the message I want people to hear, that there's more than catchy songs released as singles. The album [tracks] should get more attention. That's why Ed Sheeran is so inspiring—it's not just about pop songs."

Niall Horan:

"Getting to write and record with Ed on our album [*Up All Night*] was an honor. We need a ginger guy in the group. The closest thing we have is an Irish guy, me!"

ED SHEERAN—CAT MAN!

Believe it or not, a cat named Monty once interviewed Ed for the online magazine *Coup de Main*. Unfortunately, Monty got a bit bored with the Q&A about halfway through and wandered away, but here is some of the Cat-erview . . .

Monty: What magical powers do you imagine cats to possess?
Ed: I'd say the magical power that cats possess is always landing on their feet, I guess, and being able to do absolutely nothing and still command.

Monty: If you had nine lives, who or what would you want to be during each of them?
Ed: If I had nine lives, I don't know . . . I guess . . . one of them I wouldn't mind being me, and for eight of them I wouldn't mind being a cat. I think that'd be quite fun.

Monty: What animal is your patronus?
Ed: A cat would probably be my patronus.

Monty: It better be me. Wh was a cuter kid, you or Ror Weasley?
Ed: Um, it's probably difficul for me to say because one of them's me. So I can't real say that I was a cute kid. Probably Grint. Yea, I reckon Grint when he was that age was, yea, probably a bit cuter.

ED ON HIS BFFS

TAYLOR SWIFT
"Beautiful soul"

HARRY STYLES
"Same mind-set"

NIALL HORAN
"Irish"

LIAM PAYNE
"Head screwed on"

LOUIS TOMLINSON
"Lovely bloke"

ZAYN MALIK
"We share
similar hobbies"

FASCINATING FACTS

"UNCLE" ELTON

"Elton is continually surprising me on how much he [cares]. He'll ring me weekly just to be like, 'Don't give up. Do this single…'"

HOBBIT FAN

"I was just so happy to even be thought [of] to be involved in The Hobbit. I'm such a massive fan of all the Tolkien films and books…"

TAYLOR'S STAMP OF APPROVAL

"Whenever I finished a song [during the Red tour], I'd send it to her to get her opinion. She's… a good judge of what's good or not good."

DREAM MOMENT

"The biggest splurge I can imagine doing at this point is just walking into HMV [a music store] and buying everything!"

LEGENDARY ARTIST ERIC CLAPTON INFLUENCED ED'S MUSIC.

FIRSTS

SONG HE LEARNED TO PLAY ON THE GUITAR . . .
"Layla" by Eric Clapton

CAREER GOAL . . .
To be a train engineer

GUITAR . . .
Was given to him by his uncle

Ed thanks the audience when they give him a standing ovation!

✗ Song Choice
"I wanted raw, honest songs from the heart."

ED'S GREAT EXPECTATIONS

THE SKY IS THE LIMIT FOR THIS STAR

Thanks to everyone that has come to the shows," Ed Sheeran tweeted to fans on the night of his last concert on Taylor Swift's Red tour. "See you next year when we start all of this madness again."

At that point, Ed had already written 40 songs and recorded at least nine that would be included on his second album. So he knew exactly what was ahead for him: work, and more work! But he wasn't afraid of it; he was ready, willing, and able!

Early on in the process, Ed revealed what direction he was taking for his new album. "I think I'm gonna keep building on what I've done," he told MTV News. "Don't fix it if it isn't broken. I loved the music that I tour and play and write. I think it would be foolish to create something that I

"When I said I wanted to play Madison Square Garden . . . people said I was nuts. And I made sure I did it."

wasn't totally happy with. So I'm going to keep doing what I'm doing and building on what I've built so far."

Of course, that doesn't mean that the songs from his second album, *x*, are going to be exactly the same as the songs from, *+*. They are going to reflect the personal growth and new experiences he's had during the past year. "I guess the only challenge is finding different ways to make yourself heard and try different methods," Ed told *Billboard*. "Don't use the same ways that other artists are trying. The way I got started was instead of playing acoustic shows, I played hip-hop, soul, comedy nights. . . . Just try and find a way to stick out."

Ed has won millions of fans with his very personal and heartfelt music. Though he wants to continue to please them, he hopes that they will follow his musical journey. He will always be true to his music, but he strives to reach out and expand his vision. As a matter of fact, he admits that after touring with Taylor Swift, he's developed a real love of country music. Ed told Yahoo! Music, "Country music is some of the best-written music in the world, so yeah, one day, I would keep my mind open to doing a country record."

The future for Ed will always be centered on music—

Giving Back

Ed returned to his old school and taught the year 8 students a music lesson!

even though he once joked he might start a T-shirt and hoodie fashion line!

Ed is looking forward to getting back on the road to meet, greet, and sing for his Sheerios all over the world. And there are rumors that he will start working on his third album before and during that tour! He knows that he has put a lot of hard work into his success, but he appreciates everything that has come his way. "You have to sacrifice a lot of things to do the job that I'm doing, but I'm living a dream," he told *Coup de Main*.

And the dream will live on and on!

"I HAVE EXPECTATIONS FOR MYSELF, BUT EVERY TIME I ACHIEVE SOMETHING I JUST MAKE THE EXPECTATIONS HIGHER."

Resources

ARTICLES

Billboard, **April 12, 2014 issue**
"The Angst of Ed Sheeran"

The Review: **The Independent Student Newspaper of the University of Delaware, September 2013 issue**
"Ed Sheeran Talks Tattoos, Touring and Taylor Swift"

Teenvogue.com
"Ed Sheeran Talks Social Media, Personal Style, and His BFF (Taylor Swift!)"
www.teenvogue.com/entertainment/music/2013-07/ed-sheeran

Facts for Now

Visit this Scholastic Web site for more information on **Ed Sheeran**:
www.factsfornow.scholastic.com
Enter the keywords **Ed Sheeran**

Glossary

chords *(KORDZ)* groups of musical notes that are played at the same time to produce a pleasing sound

curator *(KYOOR-ay-tur)* a person who is in charge of a collection of art or an exhibit in a museum

EP *(EE PEE)* short for "extended play"; an EP is shorter than a full album but longer than a single

gigs *(GIGZ)* live concerts

headliner *(HED-lye-nur)* the main artist performing at a concert

lads *(LADZ)* British slang for "boys"

mates *(MAYTS)* British slang for "friends"

Index

Acknowledgments

Page 7: *Just Ed:* Edinburgh Evening News
Page 8: *Ideal Weekend:* Seventeen; *Yo-yo story:* contactmusic.com
Page 9: *Being a Ginger: J-14*; *Being bullied:* Australia's radio show Take 40
Page 10: *First guitar:* Edinburgh Evening News
Page 11: *Damien Rice concert:* The Telegraph; *National Theatre audition:* Daily Mirror; *Strict Allowance:* The Sun
Page 12: *Acting vs music:* contactmusic.com; *Choosing music:* Edinburgh Evening News; *Leaving school:* Teen Vogue; *Designer hoodie:* elle.com
Page 13: *Superpower:* bbc.co.uk
Page 14: *Remained normal:* Irish Times

Page 16: *Pay Dues:* Teen Vogue
Page 17: *Selling records:* People
Page 18: *Screams:* Telegraph
Page 19: *Open-mile shows:* Telegraph; *Jamie Foxx:* Telegraph; *Keep On Trying:* MTV.co.uk
Page 21: *Rocket Music:* Billboard; *Change look/sound:* Teen Vogue; *U.S. fans:* omg.yahoo.com
Page 22: *Label signing:* BBC Blast; *Sweet Tweet:* Capitalfm.com
Page 23: *#1 Tweet:* DigitalSpy.com
Page 25: *Writing his songs:* MTV News; *Writing what he wants:* NPR
Page 26: *Taylor's tour:* MTV News; *Elton John/Grammys:* MTV News; *Teen Choice:* Capitalfm.com

Page 27: *Second album:* Billboard; *New direction:* MTV news; *Fame/Fortune:* Hollywood Life
Page 28: *Taylor-Made:* Rolling Stone
Page 29: *Personal songs:* Buzznet
Page 31: *Performing at 2013 Grammys:* Billboard
Page 32: *Weirdest place:* Huffington Post; *24/7 schedule:* Buzznet
Page 33: *Cat person:* Buzznet; *Taylor Swift's cat:* teen.com/People; *Rupert Grint:* The Sun
Page 35: *Guitars:* People.com
Page 36: *Taylor Swift:* www.sugarscape

Page 37: *Elton John:* 10 com/ABC News Radio; *Tomlinson and Niall H* Daily Star; *Demi Lovato* MTV News
Page 38: *Cat Man:* Cou Main online magazine
Page 39: *Ed's BFFs:* J-14
Page 40: *"Uncle" Elton:* People.com; *Hobbit Fa* yahoo.com; *Taylor/App* MTV News; *Dream Mor* Just Jared Jr.
Page 42: *X song choice:* Rolling Stone
Page 43: *Thanks fans: l* night of Taylor Swift's R tour; *Building on what done:* MTV News; *Madi* Square Garden: Rolling Stone
Page 45: *Expecations:* P online magazine

About the Author

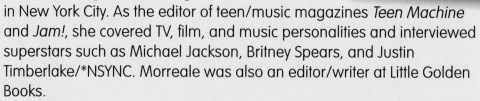

Marie Morreale is the author of many official and unofficial celebrity biographies. She attended New York University as an English/creative writing major and began her writing and editorial career in New York City. As the editor of teen/music magazines *Teen Machine* and *Jam!*, she covered TV, film, and music personalities and interviewed superstars such as Michael Jackson, Britney Spears, and Justin Timberlake/*NSYNC. Morreale was also an editor/writer at Little Golden Books.

Today, she is the executive editor, Media, of Scholastic Classroom Magazines and supplies the editors with content on pop-culture, sports, news, and special events. Morreale lives in New York City and is entertaine daily by her two Maine coon cats, Cher and Sullivan.